SECRETS OF

SIX-FIGURE

TRANSLATORS

OANA MARIA SOFRONOV

CONTENTS

ABOUT THE AUTHOR

Oana Maria Sofronov is a sworn English to Romanian translator & interpreter, mentor and successful entrepreneur based in London, UK.

She holds a Bachelor of Laws and a three-year diploma in International Relations and European Studies from Spiru Haret University in Bucharest, Romania.

A few years after her graduation she obtained the CIOL Diploma in Police Interpreting and started working as a face-to-face interpreter for courts, prisons and the National Health Service in the UK. She has also provided telephone and conference interpreting services for various companies in the US.

In 2017-2018 she worked with some of the largest creative production & localisation companies like Hogarth Worldwide and Deluxe. With over 10 years' experience of the translation industry, at the end of 2018 Oana Maria moved on to start City Translate which quickly became a reputable translation agency within the legal and marketing sector in the UK.

LINGUIST vs TRANSLATOR

A **Linguist** is a specialist in linguistics, someone who studies the language from a scientific point of view.

László Varga in *Introduction to English Linguistics – A companion to the Seminar*, describes the linguist as *"...a person who is professionally engaged in the scientific study of some aspect of language (i.e. of one particular language or of several languages or of human language in general)."*

The linguist analyses the structure of the language, which may include:

- Phonology
- Morphology
- Syntax
- Semantics

"The goal of linguistics is to provide valid analyses of language structure. Linguistic theory is concerned with establishing a coherent set of independent principles to explain phenomena in language."
Raymond Hickey - The Neat Summary of Linguistics

From these definitions we understand that someone who can speak several languages is not necessarily a linguist and, even if most linguists are multilinguals, they are not necessarily translators or interpreters.

A **Translator** converts written information from one language (source language) to another (target language). He/she is a global ambassador offering services to an ever-increasing market.

Another definition describes translation as:

> *"...finding the closest natural equivalent meaning in the target language by retaining the semantic and stylistic equivalence to blend grammatical structures and cultural contexts. The translator is like a tight rope walker, balancing these various elements in order to get the most appropriate equivalence."*

According to J.B. Casagrande, *"In effect, one does not translate LANGUAGES, one translates CULTURE..."*

With these definitions in mind, we will refer in this book to the profession of translation, and to translators as opposed to linguists.

YOUR FIRST STEPS TO SUCCESS

Before reading the book, I suggest you take a few very important steps that are essential in becoming successful.

The first step is to ask yourself who your ideal client is. You want to have a clear understanding of who you will be selling your services to, so let's identify your ideal client by answering the questions below:

1. **What do they do?** Is it a solicitor's office? Is it a pharmaceutical company?...
2. **What products do they sell or what services do they offer?**
3. **Are they a small company or a large corporation?**
4. **Where are they located**? Are they local or international?
5. **What would be their preferred form of communication**? This will help you understand how to contact them.

6. **Why would they need my services**? Determine what benefits will the client be seeking when using your services.

7. **What problems can I solve for them**?

ACTIVITY 1:

Who is your prospective client? Be realistic in your answers. You can also add company names to be more specific.

_____

_____

_____

_____

_____

_____

_____

_____

_____

_____

_____

_____

_____

_____

_____

_____

_____

Now that we have identified who your ideal client is, **the second step** is to perform a thorough market research analysis.

This is essentially formed of four areas: service, price, promotion and place.

Service

This includes all aspects of the services you provide:

- **Customer needs** –What problems can you solve for your potential clients?
- **Usage** – How or for what purpose will your service be used?
- **Competition** – What are other translators doing to attract clients?

Price

This is your pricing strategy, which will vary according to your area of expertise, location and language combination.

When doing your research, you might want to address the following types of issue:

- The value of your service to the client
- The rates your competitors are charging
- The price sensitivity of the service within the target market
- Types of discounts offered
- Established price points in the market

Promotion

This section covers everything to do with how and where your service is promoted:

- How your competitors promote their services and how that influences your choice of promotional activity
- What budget you can allocate for marketing

Place

This refers to where your services are sold: online, directly to clients or through agencies, etc.

ACTIVITY 2:

YOUR PLAN FOR SUCCESS

Take some time and think about what your freelance translation business will look like in three years. How much money will you be earning? How many clients will you have? What will a typical day at work look like? Try to be clear and give as much detail as possible.

_____

_____

_____

_____

_____

_____

_____

_____

_____

_____

I am planning to achieve this by:

Date: Signature:

Now, from a business perspective, write where you want to be one year from now. Set clear and achievable goals.

_____

_____

_____

_____

_____

_____

_____

_____

_____

_____

_____

_____

_____

_____

_____

I am planning to achieve this by:

Date: Signature:

Finally, let's write down what you want to achieve in three months from now. Think of the bigger goals you set in the one-year and three-year plans. What can you do in the next three months to get closer to these goals? Taking into account your current workload, clients and availability, what would be the best strategy to achieve your goals?

_____

_____

_____

_____

_____

_____

_____

_____

_____

_____

I am planning to achieve this by:

Date: Signature:

PRIORITIES

After clearly identifying your goals, let's prioritise five of your most important objectives you want to achieve in the next three months.

1	
2	
3	
4	
5	

THE MINDSET FOR SUCCESS

Persistently marketing your services to the right client, offered at a correct price, with the right mindset and the confidence that you will close the deal is what will make you successful and bring you close to the six-figure income (in euros, dollars or pounds).

Your mindset and thoughts dictate your success. It is essential to develop confidence in your services from the very early stages. As everyone has the ability to succeed, what eventually differentiates us is mindset and the drive to succeed. There is a place in the market for your services, and even if the quality of your work is not where you would like it to be as you are still learning or trying to make your way in the industry, it will eventually reach your expectations if you put your mind and effort to it.

My favourite passage from *The Dhammapada* – a collection of sayings of the Buddha – has been translated from Pâli as *"We are what we think. All that we are arises with our thoughts. With our thoughts we make the world."* There are various translations of this text and unfortunately I don't have the ability to determine which is the correct one. However, I prefer this English adaption as it is more meaningful and clear then the others. In my opinion, it applies to translators as: think that you are successful and your thoughts will materialise.

As translators, we come from different backgrounds and cultures, and one of the factors that has an impact on the way we think is the language we speak. According to Lera Boroditsky – a cognitive scientist and professor in the fields of language and cognition, and one of the main contributors to the Theory of Linguistic Relativity – our language shapes the way we think. With this hypothesis in mind, I tried to identify in my native language (Romanian) what words are used to describe someone successful, what gender is used most when mentioning success, how strong or empowering the adjectives that describe success are and how proverbs or superstitions affect my business decisions. For example, it has been to my colleagues' amusement to admit that I am more confident in a business meeting if I have an itchiness on my right palm on that day, as according to an old Romanian superstition "you receive money if your right palm is itching and you give money if the left one is". Also I realised that many sayings are more related to hope or "God's will" than to one's determination, and a reluctance to make more money can be easily connected to old Romanian sayings that can be translated as "Money is the Devil's eye", "Too much wealth fools people" or "With money you can buy a bed but not your sleep".

One way to alter the way language impacts our everyday decisions or mindset is to identify the negative perceptions and replace them with positive ones. At least, this is what I am still working on doing...

ACTIVITY 3:

What are the most empowering words or sayings in your native language that will motivate you or make you feel more confident?

1	
2	
3	
4	
5	

What are your top five qualities as a translator

1	
2	
3	
4	
5	

HOW TO CHOOSE YOUR SPECIALISATION

Providing general translation services is not enough anymore, especially not in language combinations where there is much competition.

There are several factors you should take into account before choosing your area of specialisation:

- What you are passionate about
- The market demand
- What you need to do in order to specialise in that field

Below is a brief description of the specialisation paths you can choose as a translator:

1. Audiovisual translation (Multimedia translation)

Audiovisual translation implies the use of a multimedia electronic system in the translation or transmission process, either at the production or post-production stage.

Types of Audiovisual Translation:

- Subtitling
- Media Accessibility (subtitling for the deaf, live subtitling, audio description)
- Dubbing
- Voice-over
- Multimedia localisation

Here of course there are many subdivisions. You can provide subtitling translations only for a certain type of documentary or film, or you might be more inclined to work with a certain genre, etc.

2. Financial & FinTech translation

With the world continuously evolving and technology always changing and improving, the financial industry is also moving towards more technical content (hence, FinTech). The skills of translators in this industry will therefore have to adapt somewhat as well.

Some of the content required to be translated by a financial translator:

- Accountancy books
- Bank statements/activity
- Business plans
- Financial reports
- Insurance documents
- Sales forecasts
- Stock market documents
- Tax documents
- Cryptocurrency
- Bitcoin documentation

This specialisation includes all the related subdivisions:

- Accounting
- Auditing
- Banking
- Business/Commerce
- Financial markets
- FinTech
- Insurance
- Investment/Securities
- Tax

3. Legal translation

Unlike the other specialisations, for legal translations there is usually a strict policy or rules and regulations in place to determine how these documents are to be translated and by whom.

In certain countries, for example, Italy, Romania, Spain, Argentina, Greece, etc., translations for the legal sector and any official documents have to be translated by sworn translators, bearing their official stamp and signature.

If you are planning to become a sworn or certified translator you might want to contact your local Ministry of Justice, Ministry of Foreign Affairs or Translators' Association for more information about the exams or study path.

In the US the translation industry is largely unregulated and they often use "certified translator" to refer to a certified member of the ATA (American Translators Association). The ATA website has more information and guidance on how to provide certified and notarised translations in the US.

In the UK the situation is very similar, and "official" translations can be provided by a translator who is a CIOL or ITI member.

Type of content to be translated:

- Contracts
- Patents
- Taxation & Customs documents
- Court orders
- Immigration documents

4. Marketing translation

Marketing is a very challenging field and usually requires a lot of communication with the client along with research and brand materials to read before translating. A translator in this field of specialisation has to be able to adapt their style of writing and tone of voice to the brand tone of voice and the client's requirements.

As opposed to other types of specialisation where the translation has to be identical to the original, marketing translations usually require creativity.

Most of the marketing content that requires translation contains wordplay (particularly puns), idioms and colloquialisms that are not easy to translate. Many might not even have a direct translation into your native language, so this type of content can require hours of research prior to its actual translation.

Types of marketing translation:

- Offline content (brochures, leaflets, magazines, press releases, newspapers, etc.)
- Online content (social media campaigns, etc.)
- Multimedia storytelling
- Transcreation
- SEO (Google Ads, keyword research, landing pages)
- TV commercials
- Brand research

5. Medical & Pharmaceutical translation

Medical and pharmaceutical translations are in high demand.

In certain cases, in order to provide medical translations you will need a certification, and this can be obtained from various institutions such as the National Board of Certification for Medical Interpreters or MiTio (the Medical Interpreting and Translating Institute Online).

Some of the subjects are:

- Biotechnology
- Clinical research
- Cardiology
- Dentistry
- Health care
- Medical devices
- Pharma

Type of medical content to be translated:

- Clinical trial documents
- Data sheets
- Drug registration documents
- Discharge summaries
- Patient information
- Product labels
- Research papers

- Toxicology reports

6. Poetry and Literature translation

If you are thinking about specialising in literary translation, you are looking at translating:

- Articles
- Books
- Plays
- Poetry
- Religious texts
- Stories

There are many organisation for literary translator that provide support and that could put you in contact with editors or fellow literary translators. They include the British Centre for Literary Translation, the American Association of Literary Translators (ALTA) and PEN International.

7. Technical translation

Technical translation covers many kinds of specialised text:

- Equipment catalogues
- Operation instructions
- Product specifications

- Software & interfaces
- Technical documentation & manuals
- User manuals

Technical translations are applied to subject fields like:

- Aviation
- Architecture
- Automotive
- Chemistry
- Computers (Hardware & Software)
- Cosmetics
- Electronics
- Engineering
- IT
- Manufacturing
- Oil & Gas
- Transport

The type of content a technical translator deals with is highly specialised and complex, and detailed knowledge is required to perform the translation of such texts. Therefore companies are usually looking to work with translators who hold at least a Bachelor's degree. You do not necessarily need to be an engineer to translate such texts, but you will have to prove extensive knowledge or experience in the field in order to secure projects with agencies or direct clients.

What is your passion?

Now that you have an idea of potential specialisations, think of which content you would be more comfortable with. You could spend a few days trialling translating different types of content. For example, if you think you would like to translate pharmaceutical content but you have never done it before, find a medical prescription and try to translate it. It will not be easy but at least it will give you an idea. The same with any other specialisation. Try translating different content for a couple of days, and see where your preferences and strengths lie.

ACTIVITY 4:

My preferred field of translation is:

_____

_____

_____

My selected strategy for specialisation/improvement is:

_____

_____

_____

_____

_____

My action plan is:

_____

_____

_____

_____

_____

_____

_____

_____

_____

_____

I am planning to achieve this by:

Date: Signature:

The market demand

When choosing your specialisation it is advisable to do some research about the latest trends or read articles about where the market is heading in the next few years. You can find very insightful market research reports on www.nimdzi.com.

It is very important to understand and know your market from the very beginning. Your location and the demand and opportunities in your area will also have to be taken into account.

A way to test the market demand is by **using Google's Keyword Tool** to perform a search for keywords related to your service.

For example, if you are considering providing legal translations from Italian into English and you live in London, UK, the search keywords would be something along the lines of:
[legal Italian translator London]
[certified Italian translation London]
[Italian document translation]

Try searching for as many words as you can think people would look for when needing a service similar to the one you are intending to offer. Everyone uses search engines so this might be a very exact and quick way to find out what the market demand is in a particular domain and area.

Another way of testing the market demand is by **checking your competition**. This is a free and quick option that can give you an insight on how well companies or other freelance translators are doing.

1. **Do your competitors have a strong social media following?**

Check out their LinkedIn, Twitter or Facebook/Instagram accounts and see how many followers they have and how engaged they are with their audience.

2. **Are there more translation agencies than freelance translators advertising for that particular niche?**

3. **How long have they been in business for?**

4. **Can you find any reviews of your competitors' services?**

Reading the reviews is very important as it will give you valuable information about your competitors, what they are doing right or wrong and an idea of the demand (if you find many reviews of a similar service this is usually a good sign, as it means there is a demand).

Basically, when doing research, you are looking to find a profitable niche that you would like to translate content for and where you can access the training and information that will lead to you becoming a specialist in the field.

ACTIVITY 5:

After identifying your potential competitors, write down what you know about them. Can you identify their strongest or weakest points? Do you know how much they are charging for their services? Is there a service you can provide that will differentiate you from your competitors?

_____

_____

_____

_____

_____

_____

_____

_____

_____

_____

_____

_____

_____

_____

_____

_____

How to specialise?

An affordable and accessible way of specialising is by using a range of free online courses. One well-known and resource-rich online platform is Coursera. On their website you can find in-depth courses from many top universities and companies. The platform is very useful and brings together a wide variety of topics and perspectives.

Another online learning platform with a large volume of material and different subjects to choose from is Khan Academy.

I should also mention Open Culture Online Courses, which provides access to online courses, podcasts and lectures from universities in England, Wales, Australia and the US.

LinkedIn Learning is a very useful platform where you can obtain certificates from various online courses and then publish them on your LinkedIn profile.

Search the internet and see what is available in your chosen specialisation, and check with your local universities too in order to see if they hold any relevant seminars or courses.

Mentors may be helpful, and there are organisations that will offer support and connect you with a suitable mentor. Some of these are free, while others will charge for membership.

A mentoring programme usually lasts 3-12 months and involves monthly face-to-face or e-meetings where you discuss your career plan, your progress, how to gain more experience as a translator or how to specialise in a certain field.

ProZ.com publishes a list of active mentors on their website where you can request mentor services directly or, if you are an ATA member, you can apply to become a mentee to one of their registered translators. CIOL has a mentoring program as well where you can receive guidance and advice on how to start your career.

Thesuccessfultranslator.com this year started a mentorship programme where applicants work closely with mentors to increase their client list and also to receive guidance with their marketing or self-developing plans. The website only accepts a limited number of applicants each year and registration usually starts a few months in advance. The website is also running a non-language-specific mentorship programme for translators wanting to learn more about transcreation.

More specialised mentoring programmes are also available for literary translators. For example, ALTA (the American Literary Translators Association) last year offered four mentorships – one for each of Polish and Russian prose, one for non-language-specific poetry and one for non-language-specific prose – where the translator could choose a project to complete within a year and receive from their mentor advice specific to that particular project.

ACTIVITY 6:

List five things you would like to learn from a mentor:

1	
2	
3	
4	
5	

THE CV OF A TRANSLATOR

The secret of a successful CV is **customise, customise, customise!**

All agencies and translation job requirements are different. What one client or agency sees as an essential requirement for a particular project, will not necessarily be viewed in the same way by another. When you apply for jobs or translation projects make sure you customise your CV accordingly.

CVs can be written in a number of ways. You can write a **chronological CV,** which means listing your qualifications, education and employment history in date order, starting from the most recent.

You can choose to have a **skills-based CV.** That means you will mention your top skill categories and provide specific examples:

technical writing, certified translator, etc. A skills-based CV is the model I recommend for translators as it makes it easier to underline your attributes and increase your chances of being contacted by agencies. You can combine the skills-based CV with a chronological list of your education/employment.

Another idea would be to create an **interactive CV**. This method can be quite efficient for those looking to work with creative agencies/direct clients. You could create a short film highlighting your skills and strengths and make it available on Youtube or Vimeo.

When writing your CV, keep it short and clear and include only relevant experience.

I do not recommend copy-pasting your CV into the body of the email. I have seen this done by a few translators, however it is ill-advised for the following reasons:

- Whoever opens the email and sees such a long message will probably give up reading it after the first few words;
- A CV is very difficult to follow in an email as the formatting is lost. Therefore, your chances of anyone reading it are second to none;
- If you believe that agencies are not reading your CV because they might think your attachment could contain viruses, then try sending a short email (200-300 words maximum) briefly describing what services you offer and

how you can help them, and state that you will be happy to send them your CV or fill in any application forms, should they require it.

What to include in your CV:

1. Language combination

It is very important to mention your language combination clearly, at the beginning of your CV and don't forget to specify which is your native language as well. Always include this information in your subject email, in your CV and in any other type of marketing material you send to a prospective client.

2. Specialisation or type of content you translate

It has been long maintained that a translator cannot handle every type of text in every industry and be equally competent in all. And I could not agree more. Nobody can be a successful lawyer, doctor, aircraft technician, IT data analyst, financial advisor, civil engineer, pharmacist and marketing advisor at the same time. The same reasoning applies even more strongly to translators. You cannot be familiar with the terminology and understand the technicalities of every type of text – in at least two languages. That is why, if you want to be successful – especially in languages where there is very high competition, **you need to specialise.** For rare languages or languages that are not in high demand, a specialisation is not always necessary. This is due to the fact that there is less likelihood of very specialised content that requires translation and even if it is needed, the client will accept the best of those available. This takes us back to the chapter where I mentioned that market research is essential for having a clear understanding about your market's needs and how you can supply that need.

If you do translate on more than one subject, and the fields are very different, for example if you specialise in marketing and legal content or pharmaceutical and literature, I advise you to have separate CVs for each specialisation. You can mention in both that you also translate the other type of content, however your main focus in the CV will be the specialisation for the job/project you are applying for.

If you are a beginner translator, you should consider what type of content you would like to translate: technical, medical, legal, etc. If you have limited experience, you can list in your CV your field(s) of interest and give clear examples of what you are doing towards specialising in a certain area, for example, attending webinars, courses, etc.

3. Education

The essential information to include in this section is your degree(s) and certifications.

Mention the name of the school you attended or the award body. You can include the country and year you graduated as well, however that is not essential.

Project managers and recruiters usually check this section; therefore, add here any translation certifications you might have, and any relevant courses you attended or diplomas you obtained. Keep this section short and relevant.

4. Membership

When writing your CV, I would suggest mentioning if you are a member of a professional association. This is very important, especially if you are trying to work with more reputable agencies.

There are many benefits to joining a professional body, from professional recognition to discounted insurance, software packages or books. Fees vary from one country to another, and from one professional association to another. Below is a short list of some of the most popular international associations you might want to check out:

- ATA – American Translators Association
- ITI – Institute of Translation and Interpreting
- CIOL – Chartered Institute of Linguists
- TA – The Translators Association
- GALA – Globalization and Localization Association
- ELIA – European Language Industry Association

- IAPTI – International Association of Professional Translators and Interpreters
- APTS – Arab Professional Translators Society
- IMIA – International Medical Interpreters Association
- IFT – International Federation of Translators

You could always check with colleagues working in similar specialisations and language combination to find out what works best for them.

Memberships not only help you build more credibility but also help you expand your professional network through local events or online groups. Many organise webinars, networking events and conferences that you can attend. This will help you learn about the latest trends in the industry and also help you get to know other translators like yourself. Some associations even have a public database which facilitates your being noticed or contacted by potential clients.

5. Recent projects

Your CV needs to clearly tell your prospective client about any similar projects you have worked on and how qualified you are to translate content in their specialisation.

I suggest you give basic details such as the name or type of project. Here is a short example:

Recent projects:

1. "[Book name]" by [name of the author] – IT – proofreading, 50,000 words
2. Financial statements – EN>IT – 35,000 words
3. Two EU financial law projects – EN>IT – 50,000 words

For more details about my recent projects and to hear what my clients have to say about my work, please check out the Project History section on my ProZ.com profile:[insert link here]

This section is very important as you can highlight any projects that you worked on that might be particularly relevant to the end client's needs.

6. Pro-bono or voluntary language services

Volunteering can be a good way of starting as a translator or gaining experience in a certain domain. If you provided such service you should mention it in a special section called "Volunteering experience".

When it comes to pro-bono translation services, the most well-known source of work is Translators Without Borders, a non-profit organisation offering language and translation support for humanitarian and development agencies and other non-profit organisations on a global scale.

TED Translators and Transcribers is a global community of volunteers who subtitle TED Talks. TED is a good place to gain experience in translating subtitles if you are looking to specialise in this field.

Another option could be reaching out directly to aid organisations, NGOs or maybe the local church.

This section can also include any other volunteering work that you have done that might be relevant for the project – anything that can show you are working towards a specialisation or that you have knowledge in a certain domain. Once again I would like to emphasise that this section should be present in your CV only if it contains information that is relevant to the project or the client's needs. Keep it as succinct as possible if your CV already shows you are experienced, and make it more detailed if you are a novice in translation or in a certain field.

7. Articles or papers published, presentation, conferences

You can include any articles or papers you have published in your specialisation area. This will show the potential client that you have the knowledge and recognition for them to trust you with their work.

Be they publications or presentations, only include them if they are relevant and only give detailed information if, for example, you presented a paper on the particular topic that a client requires.

8. Other languages spoken

Languages that you speak but do not use as working languages can help in certain projects, for example on projects containing references or foreign names. I would suggest briefly mentioning them in your CV if your level is reasonably high.

9. Other services

This section is very important as any additional services you offer may help you stand out from your competition. Here you should include services like proofreading, post-editing, DTP, transcription, voice-overs, or any other service you believe might be required by the client. Always do your research before contacting a client so you have an idea of how you can add more value.

10. Software used

The CAT tools section should always be present when applying for work with translation agencies, although direct clients will be less interested. If requested to send your CV by a direct client, bear in mind that the type of software we use is known within our industry but it might sound very confusing to someone on the outside. What you could mention instead is that you use certain tools which, should the client use your services, will save them money in the long term and make their brand consistent.

11. Work method

You could add this section in your CV to briefly explain your processes, payment terms, minimum charges applicable, your daily output and your availability for test translations.

Here is a short example of what this section could look like:

Work method

I only translate into my native language and I only accept jobs in my field of expertise where I am confident that I fulfil the client's specific requirements and can deliver the project on time.

All my translations are thoroughly spell-checked, proofread and delivered in the requested format.

I always conclude a services contract with my clients and start translating only after the receipt of a purchase order specifying all the project details.

All correspondence with my clients is treated confidentially and I agree to sign a non-disclosure agreement should you so require.

I am available for translation tests of up to 300 words and, upon request, I can also provide samples of previous translations.

As I am always striving to improve my services, client feedback is always welcome.

Please note that I charge a minimum fee of 20 EUR. This is to cover my time with any communication and research done for the project.

Availability

Monday - Friday

09:00-18:00 GMT +1

Output

2,500 source words per day for translation tasks

4,000 source words per day for proofreading tasks

Payment methods

Paypal, Bank transfer

12. Suitable format

Thorough research should be done before sending your CV to translation agencies based in another country. Many countries have different requirements and it is essential to be aware of these if you want your CV to be taken into consideration.

Name

In the US, your CV is called a "résumé", therefore when sending emails to companies in the US you should say "Please find attached my résumé", as opposed to "Please find attached my CV" as you would say in the UK.

Format

Also, the format is different from one country to another. While some countries will expect you to have a CV in reverse-chronological order, or a Europass format, others would expect you to produce a skills-based CV.

Style

While using strong adjectives like "outstanding", "excellent" or "great" can work in the UK and US when describing your skills in your CV, some European countries might dislike applicants boasting about their qualities and would prefer to see a more "practical and real" side of your CV.

Length

In the UK and some other countries your CV should be no longer than two pages. However, certain European countries prefer either a one-page CV or one that has at least three pages. Always do your research well and customise your application.

Photo

If you choose to include a photo in you CV, even if this is not required in many countries, ensure that it is a professional photograph, perhaps using the same photo you use for your LinkedIn or ProZ.com account.

Contact details

It is important to add your country of residence in your CV, mostly because this is how agencies will know when to contact you. Time zone is very important, especially when working with agencies worldwide, as this has an impact on deadlines and communication.

Even though I have seen translators' CVs that include the full address, that level of detail is irrelevant and, for your own protection and privacy, I would suggest only mentioning the city/country or region rather than the full address.

To summarise, the contact information should always include:

- Your name

- Country of residence and, should you believe it relevant, city/district/region
- Phone number in international format and/or Skype ID
- Email address
- LinkedIn or ProZ.com account or any other relevant social media or professional accounts
- Your website (if applicable).

Your CV can also include the following:

- Number of words translated so far, if you think this will increase your chances of selection and if it is relevant to a certain project you are applying to. Make sure that you update it regularly.
- Rates, to avoid wasting time on fruitless communication
- Selective quotes from client testimonials
- A professional headline that will define you or your services

CV CHECKLIST	
Contact details	✓
Country of residence and/or time zone	✓
Link to your Website	✓
LinkedIn/social media profile	✓
Link to your ProZ.com profile	✓
Native language	✓
Language pair(s)	✓
Relevant professional experience	✓
Relevant education	✓
Relevant industry memberships (ATA, CIOL, etc.)	✓
Software/CAT tools (if sending your CV to agencies)	✓
Additional relevant skills/languages	✓
Other services you offer	✓

Words to consider using in your CV: When writing your CV you should find words that best describe your abilities, experience and skills. Below is a short list of words that might prove helpful:

Accurate	Edited	Professional
Achievements	Error free	Published
Assessed	Evaluated	Proficient
Awarded	Experienced	Qualified
CAT tools	Founded	Recognised
Confidential	Graduated	Recommended
Correct	Illustrated	Resourceful
Created	Implemented	Revised
Credentials	Improved	Specialised in
Certified	Increased	Standards
Deadlines	Managed	Studied
Degree	Membership	Successful
Distinguished	Native language	Tested
Documented	Nominated	Trained

DOs and DON'Ts on a CV

DOs

- Always use easy-to-read fonts. Some of the most recommended fonts are:

Calibri	Times New Roman	Arial
Helvetica	Book Antiqua	Georgia

- Tailor your CV to the job/project description and/or to the client's requirements
- Keep the CV positive
- Place the most important information at the top
- Stay succinct and relevant
- Focus your CV on your experience (if any), on the type of text you translate/have translated, your area of expertise, the brands you have worked with (if any), and your diplomas and qualifications if relevant to the job.
- Proofread your CV or ask a colleague or friend to do it for you, especially if you are writing your CV in a language other than your native language.
- Review the Checklist on page 49 to make sure you have included all the relevant information.

DON'Ts

- Don't use strange fonts or graphics just because you want to look different or attract attention on your CV.
- Don't use more than one font and avoid overuse of italics, colours or bold.
- You don't need to include references in your CV.
- Don't lie about your experience or qualifications
- Don't use industry technical terms unless you are sending your CV to colleagues or translation agencies
- Don't include a photo unless requested for interpreting jobs
- Don't include your hobbies, objectives, age or marital status
- Don't make your CV look like a jobseeker's CV.
- Don't put every detail of your background into your CV. Its purpose is to briefly underline your relevant qualities, experience and qualifications.

Please see below a few examples of what not to include in your CV.

Objectives:

Seeking a challenging position in a reputable company where my academic background and interpersonal skills are well developed and utilised.

This example shows that you are looking for a full-time job and it should never be used. As a freelance translator, you are not looking for a job, you are looking for a partnership with a potential client or agency.

Words/skills/attributes that should never be included when applying to work as a freelance translator:

Reliable	Unbeatable service	Multi-tasker
Full-time worker	Constant availability	Proactive
Unemployed	Self-motivated	Challenging
Leadership skills	Strategic thinker	Team player

As we are talking about Dos and Don'ts in a CV, I have to share with you that the longest CV I have ever seen had nine pages (yes, nine!) and contained experience that was totally irrelevant to a freelance translator. Another CV I have read that put a smile on my face contained a full-page list of places the translator had visited, including holidays with grandparents.

To summarise, **your CV must be:**

EASY TO READ	✓
ACCURATE	✓
POSITIVE	✓
CONCISE	✓
PUNCHY	✓

ACTIVITY 7:

How well do you think you perform at the moment as a freelancer or entrepreneur? Evaluate your current situation in a maximum of three words. You can seek feedback from colleagues or friends as well and compare the answers.

Skills and performance	Self	Others
Friendliness		
Self-confidence		
The ability to manage change		

Setting & reaching goals		
Sensitivity to feedback		
Sales acumen		
Vision/Inspiration		
Networking		
Social media		
Quality		
Innovation		
Expertise		
Clarity of purpose		
Industry knowledge		
Planning		
Marketing		
CAT tools		
Attention to detail		

FEES

Let's answer a few questions to help you work towards setting your price strategy:

ACTIVITY 8:

How many words can you translate/ proofread per hour or per day?

_____

_____

How much do you need or want to earn in a week/month/year?

_____

_____

How much can your clients afford to pay? This answer is very important if you intend to increase your rates to current clients, or if you need to find higher-paying clients.

_____

_____

How much are your colleagues charging?

_____

_____

_____

Being the cheapest translator in your market does not necessarily mean you will get more projects, plus you will have to work long hours in order to make a living.

The idea that because you just finished your studies or have no experience in the industry you have to charge less is a myth and a fallacy.

Let's break it down to facts:

On average, a translator can translate 2,000-2,500 words per day. Let's try a few strategies to see which one will get you closest to the six-figure income.

If you can translate around 11,000 words/week (calculated at five working days x 2,200 words/day) your income could be:

Rate per word in euros	Weekly income in euros	Yearly income in euros (calculated at 48 working weeks)
0.06	660	31,680
0.08	880	42,240
0.10	1,100	52,800
0.12	1,320	63,360
0.14	1,540	73,920
0.16	1,760	84,480
0.18	1,980	95,040
0.19	2,090	100,320
0.20	2,200	105,600

How about if you can translate more words per week? At 14,000 words/week (calculated at five working days x 2,800 words/day) your income could be:

Rate per word in euros	Weekly income in euros	Yearly income in euros (calculated at 48 working weeks)
0.06	840	40,320
0.08	1,120	53,760
0.10	1,400	67,200
0.12	1,680	80,640
0.14	1,960	94,080
0.16	2,240	107,520
0.18	2,520	120,960
0.19	2,660	127,680
0.20	2,800	134,400

Depending on the type of client (translation agency or direct client), you might consider having different pricing strategies.

For example, you will be charging translation agencies less because they do all the end-client negotiation, they check your work and, of course, they need to make a profit.

There are several factors to take into account when setting your price:

1. Deadline

The deadline, or turnaround time, has a huge impact on your pricing. The quicker the project is required, the higher the fee. Usually, same day translations incur a surcharge or so-called "rush-fee" of 50% to 100% on top of the basic rate.

2. Complexity

Firstly, you need to assess how difficult the content will be to translate. You should always see the text before quoting. You can provide an estimate or a ballpark quote but it is better not to give an exact fee before seeing the text. If a document has a high complexity, with many scientific terms that will require thorough research, your fee and delivery deadline should be set accordingly.

3. Language combination

Your fees are also subject to the market price. Before setting your fees you might want to check how competitive your market is.

4. Word count

You need to decide if you will offer a lower price for large projects and also if you will offer discounts for TM matches and repetitions (when using CAT tools). Here is an example of discounts for fuzzy matches:

New words – 100% (full rate)

50-74% – 100% (full rate)

75-94% – 70% of full rate

95-99% – 40% of full rate

100% – 30% of full rate

For small translation jobs you may charge a **minimum rate**. This is mostly to cover the time spent on communication, reading the reference material (if any) and handling any post-translation queries. The minimum fee has to be reasonable and one way that you can calculate it is: 100 words X your rate per word plus your rate for half an hour.

For example if your rate per word is EUR 0.07 and your hourly rate is EUR 30, your minimum fee will be:

100 x 0.07 + 15 = EUR 22

This calculation is just meant as a guide to help you set your fees and not actual suggested rates.

5. Formatting

Some documents might have graphics or charts that will require re-creation. You should keep that in mind when quoting for such projects. I would suggest you add an hourly rate for formatting on top of the translation fee. Always discuss how you can adjust your fee for such projects with your client or project manager, and be prepared to negotiate.

6. CAT tools

The software you are using or you are required to use has an impact on your productivity and on the price. While a familiar tool may save time, using an unfamiliar one could actually take more time.

7. Your experience

You have a duty to continuously invest in improving your worth. You should not be charging today the same fees you charged two years ago, or that you will charge two years from now.

ACTIVITY 9:

Identify your pricing strategy:

TRANSLATION		PROOFREADING	
Lowest rate per word	Lowest rate per hour	Lowest rate per word	Lowest rate per hour

TRANSLATION		PROOFREADING	
Regular rate per word	Regular rate per hour	Regular rate per word	Regular rate per hour

TRANSLATION		PROOFREADING	
Rush job: rate per word	Rush job: rate per hour	Rush job: rate per word	Rush job: rate per hour

TRANSLATION		PROOFREADING	
Minimum fee per hour	Minimum fee per project	Minimum fee per hour	Minimum fee per project

WORKING WITH TRANSLATION AGENCIES

When you contact agencies, you are in fact marketing yourself. You should not just be sending your CV to hundreds of agencies and trusting to luck that one will contact you. You should be sending your CV to targeted agencies, ones you know work in your specialisation and language combination(s) and, most importantly, that you would like to work with.

When it comes to marketing yourself to agencies, the process we are looking at has several stages:

1. Research
2. Contact agencies/send your CV and/or cover letter
3. Fill in registration forms
4. Take translation tests

5. Professionally and promptly handle any communication

Every time you reply to an email sent by a project manager you are marketing yourself. The way you reply, how quickly you reply, how you handle feedback, how you fill in the registration forms – it is all a type of marketing and it should be handled accordingly. I will cover some of these aspects later on in the book.

1. RESEARCH

When you research a translation company you should not only check whether they are looking for freelancers within your specialisation or language combination, but also decide whether you would like to work with them.

You should think of this process as you being the one recruiting the translation agency and not only the other way around. You are the one deciding who you would like to work with, why, and whether a particular agency would be a good fit for you.

You can check the agency's website and see what services they offer. You can also visit their LinkedIn, Twitter or maybe Facebook page to gather more information about them.

It might be worth checking their reviews on ProZ.com, Trustpilot, etc., as this will help you avoid entering into a partnership with agencies who are not good payers or who have bad reviews for other reasons.

To help with your research, a list with the top 100 Language Services companies in 2019 can be found on www.nimdzi.com.

The Association of Translation Companies (ATC) has a public member directory, as does the American Translators Association (ATA). TranslationDirectory.com claims to have a list of 7,038 translation agencies, and of course I have to mention ProZ.com, with a large number of registered translation agencies as well that you can contact.

I suggest you make a list (maybe an Excel spreadsheet) of agencies that you would like to work with, and that offer services in your language combinations and area of expertise.

Below is a short example of the information you can track on the list, but feel free to add more data should you consider it necessary. Record any useful information, without adding superfluous details. If you want to optimise the time spent on your admin, this list should be updated immediately after every contact and not at the end of the day. If you get into the habit of doing so, this process will take only a few minutes, and having all that information for analysis in the months and years to come will be of great benefit.

Name & Details	Location	Contact date	Reply	Stage	Follow up
Agency 1	UK	01.05.2019	Yes	Registration forms sent	Yes 2.6.2019
Agency 2	Spain	28.04.2019	Pending		
Agency 3	Spain	03.05.2019	Pending		
Agency 4	UK	03.05.2019	Yes - late	Registered – No work received yet	
Agency 5	USA	07.05.2019	Yes – prompt	No new translators needed	

If Agency 2 or Agency 3 does not reply within 30 days you can follow up with them. Also, if an agency does not need your services now, that does not mean they will not need them three or six months from now, so you could follow up after a while and check if anything has changed.

This table is very important as it helps you analyse the response rate and take further decisions. For example, if you have contacted 50-60 agencies and barely received a reply that might mean you are doing something wrong. It might be time to re-check your CV and e-mail template or wonder whether you are contacting the right language service provider for you. You might want to call one of the agencies and ask if there is someone available to give you some brief feedback on your application. Not everyone will be keen to do so but perseverance is a key to success.

2. Successfully contacting agencies

How to send an application that will stand out?

The key is to personalise your emails and show that you did your research before sending your application. Also, you should ensure that your email or your CV answers all the questions a project manager or recruiter might have in the initial application process.

These questions are (in no particular order):

- What are your fees?
- How many words can you translate or proofread on a daily basis?
- What CAT tools do you use?
- What is your availability to take on new projects?
- Are you willing to take translations tests?

- Do you hold a certification in translation?
- What area(s) do you specialise in?
- What other services do you offer?

The email subject should include: the language combination, specialisation and/or qualification. Avoid generic subject lines like [Looking for a collaboration] or [Translation services].

Make sure you keep the subject line short and relevant, for example:

[SP > EN Legal Translator]

[SP <> EN Experienced Legal Translator]

[New Application EN>IT Technical Translator]

[Law graduate and French > Polish Translator]

[RU>EN Translator | Degree in Engineering]

[Award winning FR>IT Children's Book Translator]

Adapt and include the information that is relevant to you.

When sending your application do NOT include recommendation letters or diplomas unless you have specifically been asked for them. Your CV or cover letter describing your work method, a sample translation or a link to your website (where they can see more of your work and find out more about you) should be more than enough for the initial stage of application.

If you have a ProZ.com or similar account I recommend you include the link in your email as it will most probably be checked by the recruiter because it is just one click away.

Checklist before sending an email:	
Correct email address	✓
The subject line includes the language combination and specialisation	✓
CV is attached	✓
Name of the addressee has been double-checked	✓
There are no grammatical errors	✓
Contact details are included	✓
Link to your ProZ.com account or any other accounts where the recruiter can have access to reviews or sample translations.	✓

3. Registration forms

Translators sometimes refuse to fill in the application or registration forms as they believe all the required details are already included in their CV. They fail to return the forms, or these are dashed off in minutes complete with spelling mistakes or categories left unanswered.

This is a mistake because being sent a registration or application form is a sign that your CV has stood out.

Unlike CVs or cover letters, the application and registration forms are actually read by agencies, and often very carefully because they are part of their internal process. The information on these forms is saved in the agency's internal software and then used to match your skills to their projects, to contact you for potential jobs and to eventually pay you.

Bear in mind that sometimes registration forms do not contain all the details you might want to add, therefore feel free to add an additional sheet to the form or inform the recruiter and they will advise you what to do.

Complete the online forms offline. Type your replies into a Word file and check the spelling and grammar before copy/pasting the text into the online form.

When it comes to filling in registration forms, one of the most important section is the specialisation one. Here you will state what type of content you translate and what type of work you would like to receive. Only mention the fields that you specialise in.

4. Translation tests:

Tests are often sent out with an information pack or brief. Read them carefully and ask any questions before proceeding. Make sure you allow yourself enough time to do the test and proofread it before sending it back to the agency.

A translation test can have 150-500 words. Some technical/medical tests can be even longer and in this case it might be worth checking if you will be remunerated for your efforts.

Always check the format of the test. Translation tests are usually done offline (in a word or excel file) and usually have a comment section for you or the reviewer to leave any notes.

Why am I being asked to do a test when I have already sent a translation sample?

Translation tests are often more focused on a certain subject. Sometimes, an agency needs to test all their translators as part of their ISO certification compliance or it is a requirement of their own client's agreement. Also, some tests are sent directly to the end client for them to choose their preferred translator.

What you will be tested on:

- The ability to follow instructions
- Fluency
- Grammar
- Punctuation
- Technical knowledge
- Tone of voice – the ability to write within the brand's guidelines
- Attention to detail

5. Communication

How to stand out with an agency

Working with translation agencies is different from working with a direct client. For translation agencies, it is very important to handle communication promptly. Some translation agencies allocate their projects on a "first-reply" basis, others will send an individual email asking about availability but will only wait a short time before allocating the job to someone else.

When you are away from your computer, you can set up an Out of Office AutoReply letting anyone who is contacting you know you are unable to reply for a few hours and that you will deal with their request as soon as you are back. Do not assume that no reply will mean the project manager or account manager will know you are not available. Responsiveness is a very important criterion in the management process and account managers tend to assign work on a regular basis to translators they know will reply promptly to their requests.

A secret tip I would like to share with you that might increase your credibility with some recruiters or managers, is to have an email account with a reputable or trustworthy email provider. A Gmail account, for example, might increase your chances of being contacted over using an email address of a different provider.

Another very important part of the communication with agencies is the **handling of complaints.**

Once you start working with agencies, it can happen that you make a mistake in your translation or the tone of voice used in your work is not exactly what the client expected. How do you handle a client complaint or negative feedback?

When you disagree or you find the feedback unfair, you can politely and diplomatically explain why, give clear examples, and state why you felt it was the right decision. You can also add that you have made a note of their feedback and preference so that your translation will improve, or be more to the client's preference, next time. Receiving negative feedback or a complaint does not mean the client/agency will not work with you anymore, however how you deal with the complaint will impact your role in future projects. DO NOT ignore the project manager's feedback and always reply to the email.

If the reviewer has made your translation weaker, point this out tactfully, without criticism. Use phrases like "I noticed the reviewer changed…." or "Something the client may like to know" or "I would like to point out that…".

Below is a template email on how to professionally handle a client's complaint:

Dear _____,

Thank you for sending your feedback.

I am sorry to hear that your client was not fully satisfied with my translation. This is not the type of feedback I am used to hearing.

I accept the comments and points raised and I will make sure that I rigorously check my work in the future.

This was one occasion when the client was not completely satisfied and I am willing to work to improve my services.

Do let me know if you wish to discuss this further.

Kind regards,

Most agencies have an internal feedback policy or rating system and they will rate you on several aspects: responsiveness, adherence to instructions and deadlines, sensitivity to feedback, and of course work quality. This feedback will not always be made available to you but you can check with your project manager if there are areas where they think you might need to improve.

6. Submitting a quote to a job posting

On platforms like ProZ.com, Upwork, etc., translation agencies and companies will post their projects for translators to submit their quotes. They will give instructions regarding the deadline, type of project, language combination and, usually, will specify the qualifications, skills or experience level they would like the prospective translator to meet. Other information given can be regarding their budget or a description of who they are and what services they provide. This is an excellent opportunity to tailor your quote and CV to their requirements.

Rule of thumb: only apply to a job posting that you are competent or qualified for. **Read the job description** carefully, and check the title as well as it might include important information. Employ a sales technique called "mirroring", which involves repeating back some of the words mentioned in the job description, as these will resonate in the recruiter's subconscious mind.

For example:

Job post says: must be available to translate 2,500 words/day

CV and/or quote says: I am available to translate 2,500 words/day

It should not say: My daily output is 2,500 words

Job post says: must have experience working with SDL Trados 2009

CV and/or quote says: I have experience working with SDL Trados 2009

It should not say: Excellent Trados skills

The recruiter/project manager will scan your CV for the keywords or phrases that appear in the job post so make sure you **select from your range of skills the ones specifically described in the job post** and include them in your CV or start your quote/email by mentioning them.

Don't forget to add your fees and turnaround time for the project in your quote.

If the client already provided their deadline and budget for the project, confirm them or suggest a counter-offer.

Tips for quoting:

- Keep it short and clear
- Mention how you distinguish yourself
- Be realistic with your fees and try to add more value rather than lowering your fees
- Use any similar previous projects as a precedent in your proposal
- Talk about relevant experience and qualifications
- Follow up

What to check before submitting a quote
When is the closing date for quotes and the delivery deadline?
Have you stated your ability to deliver within the requested deadline?
Have you mentioned your fees and payment terms?
Do you know all the project requirements?
Have you responded to all the specified requirements?
Have you demonstrated your ability to translate the content?

Have you included your contact details and time zone?

Is your response in a simple and clear format?

There are several platforms where you can find work and advertise your services.

Some of these are:

- Proz.com
- Translators Café
- Smartcat
- Upwork
- Fiverr
- PeoplePerHour
- Translators town

Make sure your profiles are kept updated, you respond promptly to any requests and (the key) you always ask for feedback. On these platforms the feedback you receive is visible to all registered users so the more positive reviews you have, the more requests you will receive in the future. Set up a system to always follow up for a review from a client, especially in the early stages. On ProZ.com you can get reviews from colleagues as well so, to get started, ask a colleague to rate you and you can pay them back by doing the same thing. Positive reviews are the best marketing campaign and they cost nothing. If you receive a very good review from a client, don't be ashamed to brag about it on social media or even publish it on your website, with their permission of course. Show the world how happy others are with your services and the world will come to you.

Another idea for marketing to translation agencies is to be part of a new ProZ.com campaign called Translators of the World, where you (and your ProZ.com profile) will be featured on an Instagram and LinkedIn promotional post. This is a great initiative as you can potentially be seen by translation agencies.

ACTIVITY 10:

What is your strategy for contacting translation agencies?

_____

_____

_____

_____

How many agencies do you want to have as clients?

_____

_____

Where are they located?

_____

_____

How much of your total income will be generated by
translation agencies?

_____

_____

_____

_____

Working With Direct Clients

There is an assumption that end-user companies will only work with other companies and thus avoid freelancers, but this is not always true. Many companies, even some large corporations, prefer to work directly with translators as it is either cost effective or because they have an internal translation management team and so do not need the extra services that agencies offer.

There are a few ways you can contact potential clients, some of which I have listed in the next few pages.

First, let's start with how you can get hold of prospective clients' details.

Some of the options are:

- **Buy a contact list from a broker**

Before buying a list I suggest you check first with the broker when the database was last updated. Most services run a standard check every 30 days but it is advisable to ask the broker to run a check prior to you purchasing the list. Usually the more contacts you want to buy, the cheaper each name on the list is, however it is best to start with very specific and small selections (geographical, job title, company size or industry sector) rather than having a huge amount of data and not being able to process it.

- **Exhibitor lists**

Check out trade show websites as they usually have a directory with their exhibitors' details. You might want to check the speakers' list as well for the show, as it might contain more useful details.

- **The local Chamber of Commerce**

The Chamber of Commerce should be able to help with more information about local business and networking events or with details of other businesses that might require your services.

- **LinkedIn**

I will speak in more detail about the LinkedIn platform in this chapter, however I would just like to mention here briefly the benefits of using LinkedIn Sales Navigator.

With LinkedIn Sales Navigator you can reach targeted customers by using the search and filter option. This saves so much time because you can send InMails (message/email to anyone on LinkedIn whether they are in your network or not), so you can reach out to potential clients quicker. You will also be able to see who has viewed your profile so if a potential client checks your page you can then reach out to them.

Another benefit of LinkedIn is that you can also export your contact list, which can contain email or phone contacts (if the user has allowed LinkedIn to access this information).

- **Professional Bodies & Trade Associations**

Depending on your niche and your local area, you may be able to find details of several professional bodies or trade associations that either have a list of their members and contact details on their website or could provide details of networking events or conferences that you might be allowed to attend.

If you are providing translation services in the EU, a website that will probably save you weeks of research is The European Consumer Centre for Services (https://www.ukecc-services.net) where you can find lists of professional bodies and trade associations and filter the results by country or services.

For the US you can use the Directory of Associations (https://www.directoryofassociations.com).

The decision-maker or the right person to contact varies from one company to another. In a large corporation, for example, it is sometimes best to reach out to a marketing director, marketing manager or even HR manager. However in small companies you could contact the managing director or CEO. If you are targeting solicitors you could reach out to them directly or their secretary, the firm's administrator or receptionist. An administrator could be the contact at many small to medium size companies. You will have to assess the situation based on the details that you have and work from there.

There is a lot to do on the research side. If you are short of time or you lack the knowledge to "mine" the internet for these details but you have the budget, I can recommend sub-contracting this task to freelancers (on Fiverr, Upwork, People per Hour, etc.).

Depending on the companies you are targeting, if you are not working with a contact list you should gather around 20-40 new details per day. If you are working with an existing list then checking the information is up to date and selecting which companies or representatives to contact should take about an eight-hour day for 80-100 contacts.

Once the research side is done, you will have to decide how to reach out to your potential clients. Depending on the size of the company or the title of the person, there are several ways to contact them:

1. Cold-calling

Cold-calling is still a very effective method of contacting

prospective clients.

When you cold-call businesses you have a very short time to get your message across so it pays to think about what you are going to say in advance and to practise.

The best option is to have a script. Even if some people avoid having one, it helps you to be consistent in your message and you can then see which aspects of your message are working and which are not.

Tips:

- To sound more natural, memorise your message rather than reading it.
- Practise with a friend, colleague or family member
- The first 10-15 seconds of your pitch are the most important as that is when the person on the end of the line will decide if they are interested or not.

Example:

Hi, my name's Michael and I'm a sworn Portuguese – English translator.

I provide certified translations for solicitors and immigration advisors and I just wondered if you require my services or if you're open to a collaboration in the future.

Your response:

If they would like you to send more information:

> "That's great! Can you let me have an email address to send you the details, please?"

It is a good idea to ask for a contact name as well, to make the email more personal.

If they already have a service provider:

> "That's okay.
>
> Would you mind if I sent you an email with my contact details, just in case you consider changing your service provider in the future?"

Here, the response will usually be positive as you are offering them an alternative.

If the "gatekeeper" says the person in charge is busy and cannot take your call:

> "That's okay.
>
> When would be a good time to call back?"

ACTIVITY 11:

What is your 15-second pitch for contacting prospective clients over the phone?

_____

_____

_____

_____

_____

_____

_____

_____

_____

_____

_____

2. Emails and newsletters

Emails remain the best and quickest option to contact clients. However, email marketing has a low conversion rate due to the high amount of spam and unsolicited emails.

For a higher conversion rate I suggest you only send emails to potential clients who have supplied you with their email address or have opted into your mailing list on your website.

Tips for sending emails:

- Keep it short – no more than 300-400 words
- Say what makes you stand out
- Write short sentences and paragraphs, use bullet points, and leave blank lines between paragraphs
- Make it personal and avoid general phrases like "To whom it may concern" or "Dear Sir/Madam"
- Don't forget to include your contact details and add your website in your signature

Tips for sending newsletters:

- Only send to people who opted in
- Do not send them too frequently (once a month should be enough)
- Make them short, easy to read and relevant
- Include the option to unsubscribe
- Grab the reader's attention with the headline
- Write for your audience (write content that your audience is interested in and they would like to read)
- The design has to be simple and the colours have to be in line with your website
- Have one call to action ("check my website" or "read more on my blog" or "follow me on Instagram", etc.)

Newsletters are a very powerful advertising method if they are sent to the right audience. It is crucial to know what you are trying to achieve with this form of marketing:

- To increase sales
- To build trust with your existing/potential customers
- To educate or inform

ACTIVITY 12:

What is the goal of your marketing efforts?

_____

_____

_____

_____

_____

_____

_____

3. Direct mail (post) campaigns

A direct mail campaign is a long-term campaign that could help you reach out more effectively to those "hard to get" clients.

What you need to keep in mind here is that you will need to allocate a budget, taking into account:

- Printing costs

- Postage
- The cost of any promotional marketing products like pens, diaries, calendars, etc.

You will have to establish your budget, break down the costs and see how many businesses you could reach out to with that budget. Make a list so you will be able to go back and analyse the data.

If you want the client to be able to quickly access your website or check your LinkedIn page, don't forget to add a QR code.

What is very important with a direct mail campaign is the follow-up. I would suggest following up 2-4 weeks after the first letter, with another letter or an email.

Tips for contacting clients by email or post

- Keep it short and concise – maximum 200 words
- Make it personal; avoid "Dear Sir/Madam" or "To whom it may concern"
- Use simple language
- Explain what you do and what problems you can solve for them
- Follow up

4. LinkedIn

LinkedIn is a platform that gives you a huge opportunity to connect with business owners, professionals in your industry and people looking for your services, something that is not easy to find "in the real world".

On LinkedIn, it all starts with your profile. The headline has to clearly state your profession or how you help others, and it is most important for it to be SEO friendly so people can find your profile through Google search as well.

The summary should mention what services you provide, i.e. a description of your services, how you can help customers or what problems you can solve.

Many people will check out your LinkedIn profile after you send them an email, so it is definitely something you might want to pay attention to.

LinkedIn Learning is also a very useful tool where you can get certifications and credentials that will then be published on your LinkedIn profile.

Invite colleagues to endorse your skills or to give you recommendations and thereby build more credibility.

So, the process is relatively simple:

- Optimise your profile

- Add relevant information about your services
- Connect with people and build relationships with them by commenting on their posts.

Make sure you avoid adding random connections and only build a relevant audience that will benefit you in the long term: potential clients or people who work in the same industry as you.

You could use Linked Helper Extension to automate LinkedIn connections and messages and grow your profile quickly, while you focus on your translation projects.

I also recommend you to join interest groups where you can participate in discussions and share your knowledge.

5. Twitter

Twitter is about networking and building relationships. Try to be visible, engage with colleagues and bear in mind that social media can be a very successful lead-generating tool. Use relevant industry hashtags to have your posts indexed for other users to find you.

Encourage people to follow your Twitter account by adding a "Follow" button to your website and email signature.

6. Facebook & Instagram

These two platforms are quite different but I put them together as I have noticed they tend not be as frequently used for business by translators as the other platforms. However you should not underestimate their power and scalability. On Facebook you can create or join groups that will put you in contact with other clients, while on Instagram the strategy should be about creating visual content for your niche audience. On both platforms you can post a mixture of fun and educative content, but don't forget to sell as well. From time to time you could add a post about your services, or a good review you received. Only posting direct marketing content will result in a low audience.

7. Local networking events

Networking ideas:

- Local events organised by businesses
- Local Chamber of Commerce
- Conferences on relevant subjects
- Exhibitions
- Seminars
- Trade shows
- Speed-networking events

How to find out about networking events in your area:

- Local organisations
- Social media
- Friends and colleagues
- Special-interest clubs

Your local Chamber of Commerce will definitely be able to give you more advice on this and also help you connect with other businesses in your area.

Don't forget to take loads of business cards or leaflets with you and practise a pitch of 30-60 seconds in front of a mirror to prepare yourself to speak about your business or services. You can record yourself while you practise your pitch to hear your tone of voice or send it to your friends for feedback. There are several free apps out there to help you write and record your pitch – give them a try and see which one works best for you and how they can help you improve.

ACTIVITY 13:

What are your networking ideas? Do you know of any networking events that you could attend this year? Write down at least three ideas.

_____

_____

_____

_____

_____

_____

_____

Networking tips:

- Bring plenty of business cards or leaflets with you
- Practise a pitch of 30-60 seconds in front of a mirror and memorise it
- You can use an app to record your pitch and help you improve it
- Start your conversation by asking the other person what they do, and only tell them what you do if they ask
- Be yourself and don't try to sell
- Follow up with a short email to your new connections the next day.

8. Website and SEO

An online presence is primordial for attracting new clients. Nowadays you don't need any programming skills to build a website. There are so many platforms with templates you can use and the costs are quite low. Find a trading name or you can use your own name, add a description of your services and an "About me" section.

The "About me" page is the most important page on the website, where clients go to see if you are qualified for what they need. Here is your opportunity to tell your potential clients that you can solve their problem and how.

This page should answer the client's questions:

1. Why would I want to work with you?

2. What differentiates you from the rest?

With a little motivation, your website can be online in a few hours. You can also add a blog where you write content that will be of interest to your clients.

Always have the SEO aspect in mind: have a list of keywords to insert in your articles and don't forget to proofread your content before publishing it online. A good tip here would be to make sure that the website is optimised for mobile, PC and tablet use. Depending on the platform you use to build your website, you might need to do some extra editing so the content is displayed and optimised on all devices. Make sure you thoroughly check that it is fully functional before publishing.

A very important part of the website is the registration or subscription section. Make sure that people who access your website can subscribe to your newsletter. That way, over time you will build a database of potential clients to receive occasional announcements that might interest them, such as new services that you offer or projects that you are working on. Check out some of the available CRM (Customer Relationship Management) and email marketing software that could help you reach out to your audience and also track your marketing activity (Mailchimp, AWeber, MailerLite, MailJet, HubSpot Marketing, SendInBlue Email, etc.).

When writing the content for your website you should always have in mind the SEO. Actually, anything that you write online should be done with an SEO mindset. On wordtracker.com or keywordtool.io you can check the volume of searches for a keyword and filter the results by region. They also give you an idea on the pay-per-click rate if you are thinking about setting up a Google Ads campaign. There is also thehoth.com to help you with the keywords or Bing Webmaster Tools.

In order to track your site's performance on Google search, I suggest Google Search Console, which is a very powerful tool, together with Google Analytics. Always seek professional advice if you are thinking about setting up a Google Ads campaign for the first time. Under no circumstances set it up yourself as it will cost you a lot of money and will not bring you the results you expect.

Tips for improving your SEO:

- You can focus on local SEO by creating a Google My Business page. Make sure all details are filled in correctly and above all that they exactly match what you have on your website or any other pages. Google does not like discrepancies so make sure you are consistent and make any contact detail changes everywhere at the same time.
- Create a list of keywords by using Google Adwords Keyword Planner

- Engage with your audience and encourage them to comment or leave reviews. Google likes engagement so the more active you and/or your audience are, the more traffic you will get.
- Look for websites that will allow you to place banners or direct links on their website, as this will generate more traffic and it might help you get indexed on Google quicker.
- Check if your website has been indexed by typing on Google: "**site**:yourwebsiteaddress.com"
- Not only does your content have to be SEO friendly but so does the URL address of your website. When you set up your website, try to think of addresses that incorporate a keyword with a high number of searches
- SEO applies to social media accounts as well. Use keywords in your Facebook or Twitter posts and don't forget to add your website on your profile page and to encourage your audience to click on your website. The more people accessing your website from different sources, the higher you rank on Google.
- The content on your website has to be diverse. Try to avoid copy/pasting the same information on multiple pages.

ACTIVITY 14:

Identify 10 keywords to include on your website/blog

1	
2	
3	
4	
5	
6	
7	
8	
9	
10	

Tips for building a successful website:

- Create a website with a simple, logical, usable and intuitive navigational structure

- Make your website content-rich to attract and retain visitors
- Ensure your website is compatible with different devices
- Create an aesthetically pleasing website, limiting it to no more than three colours or fonts
- Your website needs to be fast-loading so don't overload it with GIFs, pictures and videos that are not on external links
- Use reviews and ratings from clients or colleagues
- Offer the option for visitors to register for newsletters or offers
- Ensure the "Contact" section gives various contact options (by telephone, filling a contact form, etc).

9. Referrals & partnerships

Getting referrals is among the top ways to generate more sales/leads, and it costs nothing. So, how to do it?

When delivering your services, you have to ensure you always meet and exceed your client's expectations. I know it might sound clichéd but this is how you eventually get referrals. After you deliver a project, ask politely for your client's feedback. You can provide a form they can quickly fill in, use a landing page or an email template – whatever suits you. This is how you ask your client to refer you to someone who might need your services.

Another way is to establish a partnership with another translator.

For example, if you only translate legal content from Italian into English, you might want to partner with a colleague who translates similar content but from English into Italian. Or if you only translate legal content but you have clients asking you for financial translations, you could set up a partnership with someone who provides these services. You can allocate work to each other on a regular basis or work out a commission rate, whatever works for both of you and that will eventually result in a long-term and mutually beneficial partnership.

ACTIVITY 15:

Identify five clients that you could ask for a referral

1	
2	
3	
4	
5	

What is your strategy for getting referrals from your clients? Write down a clear strategy: what you hope to achieve; how you will ask for the referral; how many referrals you aim for and by when.

_____

_____

_____

_____

_____

_____

_____

Identify five colleagues that you could potentially start a partnership with:

1	
2	
3	
4	
5	

What is your strategy for starting a partnership with a colleague? Write down why you have chosen a particular colleague; what value they will add to your business; what value you will add to theirs. How much more do you expect to earn from this partnership? By when?

----

10. Platforms for freelancers

Using a platform for freelance jobs is a great way to make extra money and to get in contact with potential clients.

Below are a few examples of platforms aimed at freelancers worldwide:

- Freelancer
- Upwork
- Simply Hired
- Fiverr
- IFreelance

- PeoplePerHour
- Guru

Are there any similar platforms in your country? Write down which platforms are most suitable for your skills and your strategy on bidding for projects. How much do you expect to earn solely from these platforms? How many new clients do you aim to get?

_____

_____

_____

_____

_____

_____

11. Marketing materials

When reaching out to direct clients, it is more likely that you will send them brochures, leaflets or business cards rather than your CV.

Your marketing material should be eye-catching and professional and include:

- Your logo or headline
- Contact details
- Language combination
- A description of the services offered

- A call to action (for example: "check my website for more details" or "click here to schedule a free 15-minute call")

My strategy One of the methods I use and find to be very effective when contacting small to medium size companies is to call them first to introduce myself. I then follow up with an email where I attach a brochure describing the services I offer. Their answer is positive 90% of the time because I only contact companies I have researched, so I know they need my services or are using another provider. My online brochure is very simple, without too many pictures or colours. It focuses more on short and clear information of the type people need from a language services provider: services offered, languages I or my company translates, working hours, what problems I can solve for them and how fast.

12. UPSELLING

One of the easiest ways to sell is to sell more to your existing clients.

ACTIVITY 16:

What additional services can you offer to your existing clients?

1	
2	

3	
4	
5	

Listen, learn, improve, repeat

You have to listen to your clients and continually adjust to fit their needs and meet their expectations.

Upselling techniques

- Provide a relevant service
- Offer more value
- Add a discount

Tips for long-term relationships with your clients:

- Ask for feedback, record any negative feedback and report back about how you will improve your services to avoid any dissatisfaction in the future
- Don't be afraid to correct a client if they are wrong.
- Advertise new services.
- Send them relevant newsletters

MARKETING TIPS FOR QUICK GROWTH

Marketing yourself means telling people what you do so many times that, when they need your services or know someone else who does, your name is the first one that comes to mind.

Marketing is defined by The Chartered Institute of Marketing as:

"The management process responsible for **identifying, anticipating** and **satisfying customer requirements profitably**".

The translation industry is very profitable, Nimdzi believes that the market could reach USD 66.5 billion by the end of 2022. There are plenty of fish in the sea, so to speak, but the question is: how do you get a slice of the market?

You can try by differentiating yourself from your competitors, so a marketing strategy should start by identifying your unique selling proposition (USP).

A USP is what ultimately sets you apart from your competitors. In order to attract the attention of potential clients, you need to find an aspect of your services that are different or particularly appealing. You need to tell to your clients why you are better.

A translator will stand out from the competition through the following:

- Specialisation
- Certifications
- Client list
- Language combination
- Experience
- Price
- Quality

ACTIVITY 17:

What is your USP? Identify five attributes that could differentiate you from your competitors.

1	
2	
3	
4	
5	

SETTING MARKETING OBJECTIVES

It is very important to set objectives (targets) and a strategy for achieving them.

Marketing objectives are generally quantitative, for example:

- To achieve a 10% growth in earnings
- To increase the client list by 10 more regular clients

How to increase your earnings:

1. **Offer your services in more language markets.**

You can reach out to clients worldwide. I have translated marketing content from English into Romanian for companies that are based in Israel, Japan and Singapore, so my suggestion would be to avoid limiting yourself to clients in your source and target markets and to try to identify more opportunities in other countries.

2. **Increase the time and budget allocated for digital marketing**

From a recent survey conducted by MarketingCharts, the most effective social ad format is:

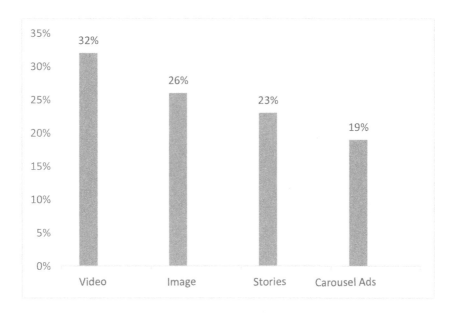

Content is king when it comes to generating leads, web traffic and brand awareness.

In terms of the marketing channel, stats show that emails and websites are considered to be more effective, followed by social media, SEO and display ads.

According to the 2018 DMA Statistical Fact Book, businesses find LinkedIn and Instagram to be the most effective platforms for lead generation, followed by Facebook, Twitter and YouTube.

Instagram is definitely the leading platform: according to marketingcharts.com, seven in ten marketers say Instagram is essential for the future.

Video advertising has seen the most growth in the past years and is seen as the most engaging way to connect with the audience.

3. **Swap your lowest-paying or late-paying client for one that pays better**

Sometimes, the best way to grow a business is to let go of the clients who are holding you back – the ones who are either not generating enough profit or are late payers – and replace them with better paying clients.

4. **Try to negotiate an increase in your rates**

It is hugely important to maintain your professionalism throughout the negotiation process and not burn your bridges with the client, as you may need that client in the future should the market hardens or if he/she may want to use your services with their new employer.

5. **Understand your existing clients and sell them more services**

The 80/20 rule, also known as the Pareto Principle, suggests that 80% of your sales come from 20% of your customers, so a minority of your clients account for the highest proportion of sales/profit.

ACTIVITY 18:

Let's focus first on those 20%, and ,try to identify who they are.

What do you know about them? Where are they located? How did you get in contact with them? What services do they require most (translation, proofreading, copywriting, etc.) ? Write down any information you consider valuable and that will help you identify their characteristics.

_____

_____

_____

_____

_____

_____

_____

_____

_____

Now that you have identified them, let's answer two more questions:

1. What services can I offer them more of?
2. How/where can I find more clients like them?

By focusing on those 20% of your clients that are generating most of your income, you are in fact focusing on growth. Ensure that you provide them with excellent customer service, deal with any complaints tactfully and promptly, and provide quality work to the standards they expect.

Now, let's try to understand what is happening with the 80% that are generating less income,

If a client doesn't generates much profit, it is because:

1. They are using another service provider as well and they only use your services for certain projects (because your fees are too high or because you are not qualified to translate the other projects)
2. They only require translation services occasionally
3. They have a restricted budget

With this in mind, try to identify if there anything you can do (e.g., add more services or change your fees) in order to get more work from them.

ACTIVITY 19:

Can you identify a client within the 80% group that you believe has the potential to move into the 20% group? Write down what you know about them and how you could adapt your services to benefit them.

_____

_____

_____

_____

_____

_____

_____

_____

_____

_____

_____

_____

_____

_____

_____

_____

_____

_____

The 80/20 rule has more powerful applications in marketing. For example:

- 80% of your website visitors come from 20% of the keywords used
- 80% of complaints come from 20% of your clients
- 80% of your sales come from 20% of your services

If the Pareto rule holds true, and you offer more services, then it would be good to understand which are your most requested services.

Example:

Michael is a SP<>EN marketing translator. He offers website and software translations in both languages. He also provides general technical and user manual translations.

Not all of Michael's services have the same demand. For the last six months, most of his income has been generated by translating websites into his native language – English. The demand for translation of software and user manuals and for translation into Spanish has been very low, while there have been no requests for the other services.

As per the 80/20 rule, we can see that Michael's income has been generated from just a small number of the services he offers.

Once you have identified which services are generating the most profit, try to focus on them and advertise them more as it is clear that that is where the demand lies. But you also have to find out why the other services are not generating much profit:

- Do clients know about the other services you provide?
- Do you advertise them as much?
- Is there less market demand?
- Are you seen as an expert in providing the other services as well?

6. Know when to scale up and build partnerships

If you have reached your maximum capacity (workload/time) then maybe it is time to find a partner to help with your projects. This can be a great way for you to increase your income and grow a successful business.

7. Choose a niche and start a podcast

Podcasts are increasingly popular and to start one you only need a computer, microphone, some podcasting software and a good topic to discuss. It is easier to produce a podcast than the content for a blog, and once you have been operating for a while and have built up an audience, you can start approaching sponsors. The most common scenario is that sponsors compensate you on the basis of CPM (cost per thousand impressions/downloads) but for a smaller niche, they might not ask for the download numbers.

8. Host webinars/seminars

Hosting webinars can be very profitable and a way to connect with your peers.

How to grow on social media for marketing purposes

First, let's set the goals and focus on just one social media channel:

ACTIVITY 20:

Which social media channel will you use?

_____

_____

What is your goal with this account?

_____

_____

_____

If you want more followers/leads, how many do you want?

_____

_____

_____

By when?

_____

_____

Who are they? Where are they located?

_____

_____

_____

How will you benefit from growing your account?

_____

_____

_____

_____

What type of content interests your followers?

_____

_____

_____

_____

How many times will you post per day/week?

_____

Tips

- Display "follow" icons for the chosen social media account on your website and email signature
- Produce original content
- Post regularly (once a day or every few days)
- Engage with everyone
- Follow/connect with relevant people
- Write SEO friendly content and make sure your profile is optimised as well
- Use relevant hashtags
- Ask people to share your posts or leave comments
- Post a mixture of entertaining and educational content

USEFUL TOOLS

FOR TRANSLATORS

Administration

How to effectively manage your admin and track your invoices?

I believe every translator should consider using client relations management software (CRM) to simplify the communication and admin side, and also to keep track of invoices and time spent on projects.

Below is a list of some of the most commonly used CRM platforms that could be very useful for a translator's day-to-day activity:

- **Hello Bonsai**
- **HoneyBook**

- **Plutio**
- **Dubsado**
- **Evernote**
- **17hats**
- **Nimble**
- **Salesforce**

Hello Bonsai has a free plan and is very easy to use, although I personally find HoneyBook to be more useful for my needs. It is definitely worth giving them a try and seeing which one works best for you. I am sure that once you start using one you will realise how beneficial it can be for your business.

Invoice templates & software

- **Quickbooks**
- **Xero**
- **Zoho**
- **Invoice Ninja**
- **Invoicely**
- **Wave**
- **Freeagent**

Collaboration tools

Collaboration tools can prove very effective when working on projects with other remote colleagues. You can create common to-do lists and leave notes for colleagues, set reminders for deadlines, delegate tasks, send private messages or video call. Most such tools have third party integrations like Google Drive, Dropbox, Twitter or Zandesk, with notifications appearing directly in channels.

- **Slack**
- **Asana**
- **Podio**
- **ProofHub**

File sharing

Sometimes it is safer and simpler to transfer files using a web service than by email. Larger files can be sent and you can choose who can see the files and for how long.

I would suggest using:

- **Wetransfer**
- **Dropbox**
- **OneDrive**
- **Dropsend**
- **Hightail**

Meetings scheduling software

It is good to have an appointments system to send reminders or let the client choose an available time slot for a telephone, face-to-face or Skype meeting.

Some of the platforms/apps I have used are:

- **Youcanbook.me**
- **Calendly**
- **Doodle**
- **Boomerang Calendar – plugin for Gmail**
- **HubSpot**

Document signature software

There are many occasions when you might need to send an NDA to a colleague, sign a contract with a client or maybe send a signed business proposal. When using a platform to send this type of document, you can easily track when the receiver has opened the document and if they signed it, and of course it gives the reassurance that the receiver cannot edit the files – they can only add the requested information and sign.

Some of the most popular signature tools are:

- **Docusign**
- **AdobeSign**
- **SignNow**
- **PandaDoc**

- **Eversign**

Social media automation

Not everyone enjoys posting daily on social media (at least, I don't) and it can be hard to find time for it when you are already swamped with projects. With the help of social media automation tools, you can put posts in a queue across different platforms. You will then have access to various analytic tools to help you track how well your posts are performing and get a comprehensive understanding of how efficient your marketing strategy is. Some platforms will even suggest the ideal time for posting or list inactive users so you can unfollow them. The use of a social media automation platform gives you access to information you would not otherwise have and the ability to post across platforms while you are focusing on your daily tasks.

I have chosen a few tools that I find to be very helpful:

- **Hootsuite**
- **Agora Pulse**
- **Crowdfire**
- **Buffer**
- **CoSchedule**
- **Buzzsumo**
- **SocialPilot**

Design & editing tools for social media graphics

If you want to create more interactive, visual and unique content for your social media posts, you might want to look at using design tools. If you are skilled in design you could create content using Photoshop or even InDesign but for more basic users I would suggest some of the design and editing tools below:

- **Canva**
- **Adobe Spark**
- **Piktochart**
- **Pic Jointer**
- **Grid-it**
- **Word Swag**
- **Pablo**

They are packed with templates to choose from. You can use some of them for free (basic features) and create content tailored for different platforms or you can create logos, brochures and even business cards in just a few minutes.

QR code generator & creator

- **QR Code Studio**
- **qrcode-monkey.com**
- **qr-code-generator.com**

- **qrcode.tec-it.com** – also generates QR codes from vCards
- **visualead.com**

CAT systems

Depending on the type of content you translate, using CAT tools may increase your productivity, help you deliver consistent translations, and build glossaries. If working with other translators, you can track any changes, and leave comments or notes. You can also check the wordcount, analyse the number of repetitions, etc.

There are many tools available with a range of different features, prices, document types that can be handled, access to online glossaries, etc. However, usually agencies will require you to work with a certain CAT tool and even provide a temporary subscription if necessary, so check that out first.

Below is a list of both free and paid-for tools (in no particular order):

- **SDL Trados**
- **MemoQ**
- **Wordfast**
- **OmegaT**
- **Déjà vu**

- **Matecat**
- **Smartcat**
- **Wordbee**
- **Lokalise**
- **Across**
- **Similis**
- **Tstream**
- **Transit**
- **Cafetran**
- **Linguee**

On their website, Nimdzi (www.nimdzi.com) have published a detailed overview of some translation management systems, with very detailed insights about functionality and integrations. Their list can be very useful if you are not sure which software to use.

Website platforms

Here are a few website builder platforms that are very popular and easy to use. You can create your website in a day, without any programming skills.

- **Wix**
- **Squarespace**
- **Web.com**
- **Site123**

- **Jimdo**
- **Wordpress**
- **HostGator**

Processing and formatting of documents

Most CAT tools will be able to convert a PDF file and provide a wordcount, but if you are not using one, you might want to look for other options online to help you convert PDFs and images into editable files.

You can use a simple online file converter to change your files in seconds:

- **Zamzar**
- **FileZigZag**
- **Smallpdf**
- **Freepdfconvert.com**

Security

As translators, we sometimes deal with confidential and sensitive information, so we need to have a security system in place.

It is very important to change passwords regularly, not to allow others to have access to your computer and to encrypt any data you keep on your personal devices.

Encryption tools encode data (emails, files, etc.) so that it is harder for third parties to unlawfully access any information stored.

Here is a short list of some of the most-used encryption tools available:

- **VeraCrypt**
- **TrueCrypt**
- **AxCrypt**
- **LastPass**
- **BitLocker**

The Three-Day Self-Development and Grow Your Business Challenge

The three-day intensive challenge contains a combination of marketing, networking and self-development, the three essentials for a successful career. It is essential for freelance translators to have a plan in order to attract more clients and to develop continuously. As the market is constantly changing, we have to do the same and keep up to date with the latest trends. Also, the challenge includes networking as an important tool for marketing.

If you follow this challenge every month for at least six months, you will surely see benefits and get closer to that six-figure income.

This challenge can be adapted, according to where you live and what options you have for networking. It has been structured in such a way that every day you have a combination of networking, marketing and self-development activities, so I advise to stick with the format.

DAY 1

- **Contact 10 potential clients**

This can be by phone, email, social media... If contacting in writing, make sure you use a template that has been proofread and customise it for the client in question.

- **Learn 5 new words in both your target and source languages**

- **Attend 1 course/webinar**

Self-development is very important for translators. Don't forget that, as a translator, you can never have too much knowledge. Attending courses is a good way to connect with other translators in your specialisation sector. If no in-person course is available in your area, you can attend a webinar or online course.

DAY 2

- **Prepare 10 posts for social media (Instagram, LinkedIn, Facebook, Twitter) or your blog**

This will help you to have content prepared for two weeks ahead. You can use one of the online tools like Hootsuite to automatically publish your content so you can focus on your translation work for the next few days.

- **Read 5 articles in your specialisation**

- **Help 1 fellow translator**

This could be by sharing a job post on social media, revising someone's CV, offering your expertise, mentoring someone new to the industry... As they say, what goes around comes around.

DAY 3

- **Add 10 new connections to your LinkedIn network**

Connecting with people from your specialisation is very important as this is how you find out about potential jobs and new trends or just simply check on what the competition is doing. You can also consider joining a new group and engaging with the members or adding new connections from that group.

- **Listen to 5 podcast episodes or watch 5 videos in your source language**.

These could be related to either translation or to your specialisation. It could be a combination of listening to podcasts and watching videos. However, make sure that the total is at least 1 hour of streaming. It is important to listen to or watch content in your source language (rather than your native one) to help you learn new terminology.

- **Attend 1 networking event/conference/trade show**

This is very important as meeting face to face with potential clients is a good way to build relationships and generate leads. Depending on the area you live in, there might be several conferences or business shows you could attend to connect directly with potential clients.

Printed by Amazon Italia Logistica S.r.l.
Torrazza Piemonte (TO), Italy

12577745R00082